Spaghetti Lenni

The true rescue story of Lenni, sprinkled
with a little extra pecorino Romano!

By Annet Artani

Archway Publishing books may be ordered through booksellers or by contacting:

Archway Publishing
1663 Liberty Drive
Bloomington, IN 47403
www.archwaypublishing.com
844-669-3957

ISBN: 978-1-6657-1585-0 (sc)
ISBN: 978-1-6657-1584-3 (e)

Print information available on the last page.

Archway Publishing rev. date: 01/07/2022

This is the true rescue story of Lenni sprinkled
with a little extra pecorino Romano!

Dedicated to my parents who taught me to love animals
and to pass that love along to my son, Gregory

Lenni wasn't always a spaghetti lover.

She was found with her kitten sisters hiding under a bush by a girl named Ini Capellini.

They had sweet little orange faces, big green eyes, striped like little tigers,

and the size of a peach, each.

Surely, she couldn't just leave them there!

She tried to scoop up all three in her arms but they were so wily, and squiggly

that they wiggled their way out.

That didn't stop Ini Capellini.

She would come back with a basket to put them all in.

"Rescue mission underway!", she shouted with excitement.

But by the time she got back, they were gone!

Just as her heart sank, she noticed an orange head peeking out of a bush.

The tiny kitty just sat there looking up at her, blinking and meowing as if saying,

"Pick me up, silly girl!"

And so she did.

By the time Ini Capellini bathed her, gave her a bowl of milk and cuddled her, she knew she couldn't just give her away. This itty bitty kitty had licked her way into her heart-

and when I say licked, she licked, and licked, and *licked*, constantly!

So, why all that licking, Ini Capellini pondered.

"Am I made out of sugar?

Am I salty?!

Am I a flavor, super delicious to motherless kittens?"

Nope! Kittens usually drink milk from their mommies, but since she didn't have a cat mom, she had the next best thing- an adoptive mommy whose skin tasted like the local trattoria!

You see, Ini Capellini ate lots and *lots* of pasta.

She had bow ties for breakfast,

linguine for lunch,

spaghetti for dinner,

and fettuccine bites in between!

Basically, *pasta was her life*!

Ini Capellini's mama, Julia, was also a pasta chef, and encouraged her pasta-loving daughter to make macaroni art in between delicious bites.

Ini Capellini's bedroom walls were covered in pasta sculptures.

Ever see a Leaning Tower of Pasta?

Or a Mona Ziti?

Leaning Tower of Pasta

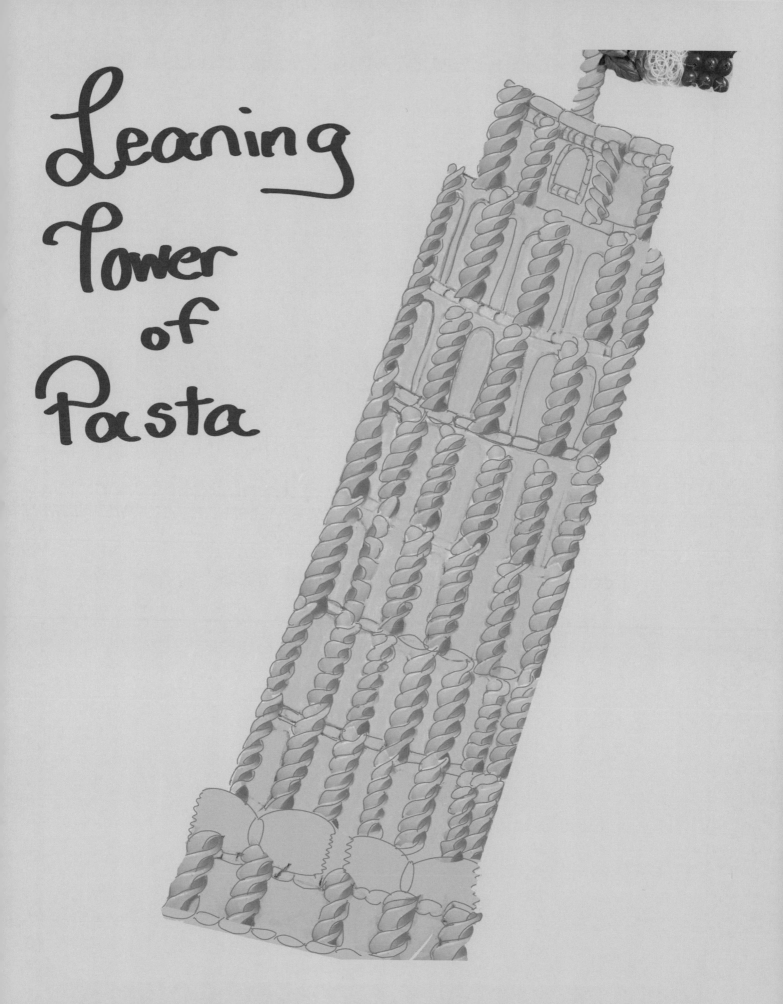

When it was time to feed the kitten, Ini Capellini looked in her cupboard and saw a sea of pasta staring right back at her and knew what to do.

"I could make a fine spaghetti with meat balls for my new friend!," she thought.

"But wait! What would I call her?" she wondered.

In the corner of her eye, she saw something shiny and bright; it was a penny being lit up like the sky on the Fourth of July by the reflection of the sun.

"Hmmmm....Penny? Nah.

She doesn't *look* like a Penny, even though she is kind of copper."

And then in that moment, the kitten started to lick her.

"I got it! Penny with an L = *Lenni*!

Because she is as *shiny* as a penny, but also *licks* much more than any!

And that is how Lenni got her name.

Her nickname was another story...

Living in a castle of carbonara soon did something to that tiny little kitty and turned her into a full blown Spaghetti cat.

As she got bigger and bigger, she grew hungrier and hungrier, and Ini Capellini worried they would soon run out of food.

"Mama, Lenni is hungry again.

I found her eating one of my sculptures!

What if we run out of food?," she worried. "Ini, there will always be a bowl of spaghetti for our hungry little Lenni," said mama Julia as she prepared more pasta.

As Lenni transformed into an extra round kitty, some of the neighborhood kids started to notice her as she meowed to them from her balcony. She was one story up, atop a tiny ledge, balancing her portly little body, meowing at the tiny, curious humans hoping they would fling a bowtie pasta from inside their pockets and straight into her mouth.

Suddenly, a boy yelled up to her and said

"Well, my, my, my...how much are they feeding you up there?"

24

Ini Capellini heard him and ran out to defend her kitty and said,

"Lenni is perfect! You're just jealous because she gets to eat yummy spaghetti EVERY DAY!"

"Then you should call her Spaghetti Lenni because it looks she's got a giant bowl of it lodged inside of her belly!" said the boy with a snarky grin.

Lenni turned her head around as if to say, "Heh?....
HOW RUDE!"

Was this boy serious? Sure, she was rounder than the other cats on the street below, but *they* didn't live in a palace of pasta. Plus, she just loved napping on her double chin and using it as a headrest after a big meal.

Each day, children would yell and point to Lenni and say, *"Ha ha, its Spaghetti Lenni!"* and laugh.

Lenni was puzzled.

"What's wrong with a little spaghetti for breakfast, brunch, lunch, an afternoon snack, dinner, dessert and a late night snack?" Lenni thought.

Lenni liked being squishy because it reminded her that she would never be hungry again.

As she realized that, she began to take the comments with pride.

"I AM Spaghetti Lenni!

But I am also large and in charge of my lasagna,

Bold, beautiful and full of fussilli, and I'm as ferociously

plump as the yummy tomatoes in my marinara sauce!"

It was from that day on, whenever the children came by and *tried* to make fun of her for being pudgy, Lenni arched her back with pride and took it all in happily, just like a steaming bowl of delicious spaghetti.

Printed in the United States
by Baker & Taylor Publisher Services